T0130135

The Book
of
Nicole

Nicole DeMario

BALBOA.
PRESS

A DIVISION OF HAY HOUSE

Balboa Press books may be ordered through booksellers or by contacting:

Balboa Press
A Division of Hay House
1663 Liberty Drive
Bloomington, IN 47403
www.balboapress.com
1 (877) 407-4847

Because of the dynamic nature of the Internet, any web addresses or links contained in this book may have changed since publication and may no longer be valid. The views expressed in this work are solely those of the author and do not necessarily reflect the views of the publisher, and the publisher hereby disclaims any responsibility for them.

The author of this book does not dispense medical advice or prescribe the use of any technique as a form of treatment for physical, emotional, or medical problems without the advice of a physician, either directly or indirectly. The intent of the author is only to offer information of a general nature to help you in your quest for emotional and spiritual well-being. In the event you use any of the information in this book for yourself, which is your constitutional right, the author and the publisher assume no responsibility for your actions.

Any people depicted in stock imagery provided by Thinkstock are models, and such images are being used for illustrative purposes only. Certain stock imagery © Thinkstock.

Print information available on the last page.

ISBN: 978-1-5043-8524-4 (sc)
ISBN: 978-1-5043-8525-1 (e)

Library of Congress Control Number: 2017912639

Balboa Press rev. date: 08/23/2017

To Rick, Angelica and Ramsey...thank you...I Love You

To those who have come before....
    And to those who will come after...
        Thank You, Your Light enlivens us all.

When I have the courage to live my dreams, it means that no one else has to.

Who decides what "Perfect" looks like?

Trust there is a way, and you
know what that way is.

What if your fear is the very thing that brought it to you? Fear can be creative. For whatever you are imagining, you are giving life to. Give your attention to what you want, and watch what you want, become your new reality.

We all have the right to walk the paths
we're walking, to be where we are,
without judgment. We even have the
right to it without self-judgment.

If your thoughts about me can have you having that experience, your thoughts about anyone can.

If an interaction <u>takes</u> more often than it <u>gives</u>, is it one you desire having in your space? In order for you to live a life you desire living, you **must** feel good more often than you don't. How does each interaction have you feeling? If it leaves you feeling poorly, more often than it doesn't, is it worth having in your life? Aren't You worth more than that? Decide that you are, then choose it.

Each moment gives birth
to new experience.

There are many different versions
of 'right' and 'wrong.' Which one
do you choose? Why choose any?

(Can something be 'right' for you and
'wrong' for another? Yes, this can often
be true. So, instead of focusing on
what might be best for another, why
not just focus on what is best for you.
You might just find yourself happier.)

Why do some equate being human with imperfection, with the ability to make mistakes? Can "I'm only human" mean something else, something which lifts you rather than lessens.....

It's always a choice to pick a good thought or a bad one. Do yourself a favor and pick a good one.

The potential danger of participating in a christian community, or a jewish one, or an islamic one, or any one for that matter, is that one might begin to think that THAT community is ALL communities and that it is representative of all people, all beliefs, when in reality it is only one community among many.

It is unnecessary to use guilt to galvanize me; I act when I feel so moved, and don't when I don't.

Sin. What is this concept called "sin?"
Who is its author, the person responsible
for its creation? Man? Why would man
condemn himself? For what purpose?
So that Man and Woman could love
themselves better? More fully?

Choose only to believe in those
things which exalt you.

Do I have to believe something 'wrong'
in order to determine it is not for me?

In terms of fidelity, am I
remaining faithful to myself?

When people tell me "No, this cannot be done," something within me ignites. Not only CAN it be done, but it Will Be done!

I'm more committed to this moment than that one; that one already was.

Each moment is new-unlike any
that have come before, and unlike
any that will come after. It is a
moment entirely its own.

If man can claim the Bible is inspired by God, then man can claim anything Is.

WE deserve to have what we desire whether we're working hard for it or not. "Deservingness" is not determined by how hard one works. Can working "hard" or "working towards" a goal be factors in their achievement- yes, they can, but they are not required. <u>Knowing</u> you are worthy of whatever you desire IS.

I use to want approval more than I wanted my dreams; now, I want my dreams more than I want approval.

Fact is only Belief accepted as Truth.

Some believe we are here, on this planet, for some divine purpose, a purpose determined by others before our incarnation here-one which we need know nothing about. Others believe we ourselves have determined our paths before being birthed...but neither of these beliefs allow for our individual choices while we are living, it disallows for the potential dynamism of each and every moment. In those beliefs, there is no personal responsibility, no ability to create whatever we want, whenever we want. This invalidates our personal freedom. Our ability and our right to be the sole architects of our lives now.

Do I believe in personal purpose, a purpose that can be decided by you in each and every moment? Yes, I do. In fact, it is the only purpose I do believe in. It honors our rights as Creative, Conscious, Self-Determining Beings.

I have heard it spoken that the Universe is for us. This I Believe. In a sense. It's will is not independent of our own. *Your will IS Its will.* So, in a truer sense... It is neither "for" nor "against;" it simply supports us in having that which we Think, Believe, Desire, Feel.

Never allow others to treat you less than You feel You deserve. Be fully committed to your worth.

Awareness is such an interesting thing-it is not necessarily that things are either this or that- it is recognizing that they are neither and both at the same time (all without the filter of belief, opinion, points of view, perspective, or story). We relate with them how we relate with them, mistakenly believing others do as well.

Having the Courage to Forgive Oneself is one of the Greatest Gifts of Self Kindness there Is.

All the Experiences that came before are Beautiful; they're what I Chose...Then. ♥

Do you want them to recognize
Your Truth or Theirs?

No man or woman has the right to decide what is appropriate for my body. I alone stand in that choosing.

There is no where you can
be where you are not.

We exist in community always
whether we are of this or not. What
ones are you most aware of?

You are part of a global community and a
human one. From a unified perspective,
we share Consciousness. So, next
time you are feeling alone, isolated,
separate from others, know this exists
only in your thoughts (the only place
it could exist, the place that thought
began). We share connection always.

Have you ever wanted so desperately to be part of something-some group, some organization, some political or religious organization-that you were willing to suspend your sense of what felt good to you? *You allowed what you hoped to be true to be more important than what was actually true?* You are not alone if you have.

(My best advice is: Pay attention to how it feels to you. Is there anything about the experience which gives you pause? If what is being experienced does not feel true to you, ask yourself what does. Is it in *your* best interests to continue (as those interests are defined by you)? What "want" are you most connected with in this moment? Are you able to get that want met while still remaining true to You?

There are always ways. Select those which honor You.

There are those who believe in
a plan greater than their own,
but what may I ask you, can be
greater than Your Own Plan?

Are you not your best
authority in all things?

Some have preferred to have others tell them what to think, what to believe, who to believe in. In fact, there are entire institutions created for that sole purpose. But, this has never been my way. My way is to choose for myself. Try it on; you might find you like it better.

Never assume this conversation is
a continuation of a previous one.
Treat each one as something new,
because in truth, it is. No two ones
are ever exactly the same.

If everything is Perfect, it
can be nothing else.

If a particular friendship comes with obligation, I'd rather do without it, in the very least, I'd rather do without that one.

I use to have friendships that came with obligation. Certain things were expected of me. I was expected to listen when they had need. I was expected to pick them up and take them places when they were unable to utilize their own means. I was expected to do things to help them when they needed help. When I was unable or unwilling to meet their needs, I was met with frustration, anger, silence. But where in this equation was space for me? What about my needs? What about my care-taking of self? Because of these previous relationships, I now choose ones that love me without expectation. I may choose to assist others, but I never feel obliged.

In Greek myth, Zeus turns himself
into a white bull, a swan, an eagle;
in Christian myth, Satan turns himself
into a snake. In both myths, beings
with extraordinary powers change
form for their own purposes and ends.
Why is one belief system so clearly
considered myth while the other is not?

(In other words, does it not strike you
as unreasonable that one would be
assumed real while the other is not.

Each moment is complete.

What would Jesus do? IF he existed, there is no way to know what he would do. I ask,"What would YOU do and allow Your voice to be Your guide.

Any time you ask what another would do, whether it be Buddha, Jesus, Mandala, or any other than yourself, you are turning away from Your wisdom. You are placing wisdom as something outside of Self. Your Self.

We are each of us innocent. What if we lived from this place rather than its other...(any other)

Why do you need for there to be a
god or goddess for you to choose
peace with your world? What could
be Greater than YOU? Than Me?

Do you only choose peace under the
threat of eternal torment? Does it
not make sense to choose it because
its opposite brings living pain?

Just because someone claims it's the word of god doesn't mean that it is. Just because someone claims there is a god, doesn't mean there is. What if the word of god was the word of you? What if the word of god was none other than the word of you? What if your words were the words of wisdom? At least for You.

Just because someone claims
its true doesn't mean it is.

What does YOUR Truth tell you?

Eve is not only responsible for Her choice,
she is responsible for His too? How
does this teach personal accountability?
She is responsible, but he is not?

What is God's responsibility in this story?
Did he not create the situation in the
first place? Did he not tempt them both?
"You can have this, but you cannot have
that." Whatever was there for either
of them to prove? Adam and Eve were
worthy of Everything, and so are WE.

We are each Our Own Discerner
of Truth. For what may be True
for Me may not be so for You.

I use to pray to a god I believe
existed outside of Self. Now, when I
pray, I realize it has been to myself
I have been speaking all along.

In christian myth, Jesus was considered the 'son of god.' And this god, said to his son, "not only will you be punished for what another has done, but you will be punished horribly, die horribly, and it will be prolonged."

What emotionally healthy parent would ever wish this on his or her child? And, what emotionally healthy child would ever agree? It lacks discernment. It is why this person Jesus can never have my faith, if such a person did indeed exist. He failed to value himself. He failed to consider what was the best of all things for him. He failed to consider humanity's innocence in all things. Such a being could never hold my interest or my faith long-lastingly. Neither could this god.

What purpose could crucifixion serve?
How could it absolve humankind for
choices not yet made? Why would
it be assumed it would be needed?
It is a punishing perspective. It is a
punitive one. These things will never
have my faith either. What if we loved
rather than condemned? Would we
feel better or would we feel less?

Just because it is written in a book, does not lend it any greater credibility than anything else. It only means, it is something written in a book. If one thing in a book is true, does it mean all things are? We are the deciders of what is True to Us Each-You for You, Me for Me.

Numerology: What if numbers were only numbers. You are the sole decider of what is True for you in each and every moment (independent of the stars, the sun, the moon, the tides, and yes, numbers). We can define our lives by them if we choose, but we do not need to. We can be as unbound as we desire. We, who are without limit, can live without this limit; we can live without this game.

When I see numbers, or combinations of numbers, I simply notice and let go without attachment to meaning or significance. I can be in that moment in Joy. Anything that wants to be revealed to me will be revealed to me. There is ease in this. The mind is free to do what it does. I am free to do what I do. No need to engage the mind. There is nothing to figure out. Life reveals Itself to Me Beautifully.

If we are to assume anything,
why not assume everything
is "for" us than against?

When anyone holds another as incapable, they are seeing this other as less than themselves. What relationship can flourish in this way? You are capable and they are not? What would that relationship look like if all were seen equally?

I am Capable. He and She are Capable. WE are all capable in our own way. This sets us each Free.

I got out of bed today; I love that. I made myself a green smoothie. I love that I care for myself in this way. If I forget to do these things which nurture me, it is fine; I will do them tomorrow or the next day, whenever I feel like doing them next. This in itself nurtures me, my soul, my spirit, that which makes me me.

If all our answers are within, why would anyone want or need to read a book, attend a lecture or a retreat, have a conversation with another? Choice. We can receive our answers within and we can receive our answers without. Both can provide us with what we need. How do you want to receive yours in this moment? Which way is your way now?

We can have an experience of time/ space, but we do not need to.

I could tell you I am always Kind,
Transparent, Authentic, Raw, Revealed,
Fully and Entirely Presenced, but the
Truth is, I do the best that I can in
every moment. It is enough, and it
is for you too. Live your life the best
way you are able. It will be enough. It
is Enough. You are always enough.

I'm interested in having women in my life who are interested in getting together not just when it is convenient for their husbands, partners, families and children, but when it's convenient for them. Pleasure for the sake of pleasure. With 'it' as 'its' guide.

Why would anyone want any of those things (husbands, partners, families, children) if it meant a sacrifice of self? Do men enter into these types of relationships with the same expectations? In my experience, most men do not. So why so with women...

Why do women refuse their
radiance? Why have I?

Choose You First. All Other Beauty
Follows From This Choice. When you
feel enriched, you are better able to
share that enrichment with others.

One Cannot Be Limited By
Another's Thoughts, One Can Only
Be Limited By Their Own.

Everything Before Us, Around Us,
Within Us is An Opportunity....

"Home" is Where One Always Is. It is
the Place Where Consciousness Resides

(There is peace in this. Safety. For wherever we go, we take ourselves with us. Home is then not a place to 'get to,' but rather a place we always inhabit. A place we cannot be separated from.)

When seeking, there is so
little room for having.

When you hold it as the only possibility,
it becomes your only possibility.

I choose you...so I could know me.

Worth is not something accorded circumstantially, but rather it is something afforded just simply by being...

The Universe does not decide whether
you can or can't-it simply says "yes!"

Life is whatever one determines it to be.

If Eve tempted Adam, who
tempted them both?

Christian story would have us believe that Eve tempted Adam, so he bears no culpability for his own choice. But, I would ask you this, in this story, who placed the tree there in the first place? Who's success is this situation designed for? Certainly not theirs.

With my own children, I do not place them alone in a room and tell them they "can <u>touch</u> everything, but this." I do not tell them they "can <u>have</u> anything, but this." What would be the purpose of this? I would be crafting a situation not designed for their best success. *I* would be the one tempting *them*.

In this story, this god is the architect of original sin; he committed all of the above. This means 'he' is flawed;' 'he' created a game even 'he' cannot win.

Love accomplishes what hate cannot.

Consciously creating a 'yes' where
none previously existed

Whatever I am wanting-give, without thought to its reciprocal receipt.

To judge another is to judge oneself.
There is nothing we are separate from.

There is great merit in being
kind, not only when it is easy,
but also when it isn't.

When people start talking about their way being THE way, I can only assume they mean for them only.

If we want the world to be different,
we have to be different in the world.

There is nothing that is denied me ever.

This world exists as such because
we have conceived it as such.

People do things when they are
ready, and not a moment before.

You don't have to know the whole
journey to take the first step.

I alone decide what is possible for me.

Regarding the Adam and Eve myth, it teaches women they are responsible for everything, and men they are responsible for nothing.

I use to think I had to process
everything in my life. I now know,
it is enough to simply enjoy it.

One can never know how any experience
may ultimately serve another. It is
best to remove oneself from trying.

One of our greatest gifts is the
ability to think ourselves in and
out of every situation.

In our Divinity, We have created nothing which is our master, unless of course, we believe that something is.

What if by checking out, you
were actually checking in...

(Removing ourselves from being in action can be the very thing we need to hear our own voice. What is yours telling you?)

Happy, Aware persons do not say, "I will sacrifice my happiness for yours." They know there is enough for everyone. They live their fullest lives and allow others theirs.

Everything that isn't Space is Energy.

If all Energy is Equal, it's neither greater than nor less than any other. It is all equally Conscious, Creative, and Relational.

It can respond according to one's belief, but that does not mean it is its fundamental nature.

If you're waiting for another to give
you permission to live YOUR dreams,
you may never live them. Decide
they're worth having, and have them.

There are those who want to be
led and those who will lead.

If you can't claim your worth, who can?

Your path is your path and
my path is mine.

Every morning, upon awaking, I tell myself, "I Love Myself"-not only because it feels good, but also because its true.

I make Self-Love my practice.

The way that I do things is the
way that I do things. I allow for my
expression in this life, because it's my
unique one which brings it value.

It is mine this world needs. It is
mine it chooses. Again and
again and again.

If you're going to commit, commit
wholeheartedly-lest you find
yourself wondering 'what if?'

In 'its' time it reveals itself to Me

Everything I am is a direct result
of Who I have Chosen to Be

Social Consciousness would have us believe we are slaves to our biophysiology; when in Truth, we are slaves to Nothing.

If your thoughts about me can have you having that experience of me, your thoughts about anyone can. What thoughts are you holding when you hold others close? For others are never further than your furthest thought. If you are thinking about them, you are relating with them. Are your thoughts about that which you love about another person or are they about that which you find wanting? If you are focused on that which is wanting, you will only see, experience, feel that which is wanting. Your relationship with others is more often about your relationship with yourself than it is about them.

How can we know one another,
when at best, we are infrequently
unaware of ourselves?

There is nothing I can do where
my love is not present for me.

People are as busy as they want to be.

What if we see what we expect to see?

What if the 'unexplainable' is only that which has not yet been explained?

I have heard it mentioned that 'god' does not abide where ego is. But, if 'god' is everything, how then is it possible for 'it' to be anything but everywhere within everything?

Someone once said to me, "I want someone who wants me." But, what if that 'wanting' left that other wanting?

(In other words, what if you want someone specifically, but that someone is unable or unwilling to treat you the way you desire being treated-with respect, consideration, appreciation, or any other quality you have specifically defined- what then? What have you gained? You may have gained the person, but not the condition of your relating. What allows for sustainable relationship-the person or the condition? The person can IF he or she partners it with the condition. Rather than define WHO it is you want, I encourage you to define WHAT it is you want. Keep that list close. You'll know when you have what it is you want because it will FEEL like you do.).

I alone can decide what is True for
ME. I AM the only one who can.

Whatever I Think and Feel is Valid.

Hold the best possible as possible

What world would we inhabit if we
each knew we were responsible
for the thoughts we entertain?

Thoughts arise, but those that have our attention, have our focus. Notice which ones you allow to have your attention most frequently. Do they have you feeling good or feeling poorly?

"I have so much to feel good about."
"Nothing I do matters."

Which of those thoughts has you
feeling better? Which thought brings
you home? Feel as good as you can as
often as you can and watch the quality
of your life change for the better.

What if "Home" is already the place we inhabit? And what if the only reason our Consciousness has chosen any of this, all of this, is for the Simple Experience of it All....

Words without action are only words

There is always a way, often many.
(This focuses one on solutions; if one
holds things as possible, they become
possible, often even probable.).

All things are possible with belief.

I have heard it spoken women cannot be president because they are too emotional. By that way of thinking, women cannot be anything (doctors, attorneys, teachers, EMPLOYED). Women can be ANYTHING, and they can be anything on THEIR terms.

(Never assume because you are
emotional another is. Never assume
emotions arise within one gender
only. Never assume emotions are a
weakness rather than a strength. Is it
not time to put these beliefs to rest?

Question them. Examine them.
Hold all others as capable and
watch what that brings you.)

Why would you want to believe
in someone or something that
condemns you, judges you, asks you
to prove yourself as worthy, offers
you only conditional love? What
would be the benefit in that?

If you're going to believe in someone, believe in Yourself. If you're going to believe in something, believe in Love.

Instead of a turning away
from Self, turn towards.

Choosing to like someone is a choice.
One you must make, often
more than once.

There are always ways, often many.

I give myself permission to have what I want, be what I want, do what I want. The only permission I need is my own.

I give myself permission to be who I am
and where I am. It is the appropriate
place for me to be. I walk the path I walk
and only I can choose it differently.

Do I lead or do I follow? Do you lead
in one way and not in others?

I have seen persons consciously choose their political beliefs, but not consciously choose their religious ones. What is it that Feels True to YOU? You are welcome to try on another's beliefs and see if they fit you, but You are not They. *Does it not Feel better to live YOUR Truth than try to live another's?*

Do I see the best in things or the worst?

People can say anything; it doesn't make it true, and it doesn't make it true in my experience.

Never assume your belief system is mine.

Your way may not be my way.

Believing in someone is trusting they
are capable in all their decisions.

My Relationship With the Universe:
My will **is** its will. My desires are
its desires. My way is its way.

When I really get that this is how
it works, there is nothing to be
anxious about because everything
I am desiring is assured.

Every relationship we enter into is a holy one-whether it is an unconscious choosing or a conscious one. It is holy because we each are holy. It is holy because it can be nothing else. We each are Perfect and Divine, and yes, Holy in our every expression, regardless of what that expression looks like. So, it is never a matter of whether it is or whether it isn't; It is ALL Holy; I allow for nothing else.

People can say anything. Do their actions align with their words? Does their Energy?

People are allowed to be one thing
in one moment and something else
in another. We get to choose HOW
we show up in every moment.

We can be as dynamic as we wish
to be. We can also be as static.

There is a danger in judging another-for whatever you judge you can become.

I Love when I command the universe to reveal something to me and it does.

If you take care of this moment, the
next one will take care of itself.

The ability to create your life rests with you; what is it *you* wish to create?

A healthy mind equals a healthy body

Instead of focusing on what
other's can do, focus on what
you can do, in this moment

(how much of what we do is about
fixing others; fix your own thoughts
and allow others to do the same)

If you're going to do anything,
do it because you want to rather
than because you have to.

I say 'yes' to those things which are a 'yes' to me and 'no' to those things which are a 'no.' My life feels better when I do.

How do we talk about our children when they're not with us? Is it with love?

How often do we assume because
something is not right for us, it
is not right for another? Let us
each choose for ourselves only

Faith is belief in the absence of evidence

Never assume you know what it's like to be another person. You have never lived another's exact experiences, you may have shared some, but you have never lived their exact ones.

If you've got nothing to hide, hide nothing

There have always been those
who have not needed others to
tell them what to do, think, and
believe. Which person are you?

Regardless of what you were raised believing, ask yourself this, does what you're reading and hearing make sense to you; if it doesn't, what does? Be willing to discover what is true for you.

If given a choice whether to look
backwards or forwards, look
forwards; it carries with it a
wealth of new possibilities.

If the law is not applicable to everyone,
how then can it be applicable to anyone?

I could teach only love, but what
would that do for my practice of it?
Do I want to only teach it, or would
I rather live it, see it, embody it?

Our country should not have our loyalty
if it is undeserving of it. Nothing should.

When we dehumanize others,
we dehumanize ourselves.

Anyone who does not consider you, does not deserve you.

I think only the best of all people
and get only the best back.

Why would anyone want to give their faith to something which condemns them? Why would anyone want to believe they are guilty of another's sin or any sin, for that matter? Would you not be better served believing in something which believes in you?

If you're going to place your Faith
in someone or something, why not
place it in Yourself? BELIEVE You are
capable of Anything and Everything!

In order to have something new, one
must be willing to do something new.

Printed in the United States
By Bookmasters